D1505796

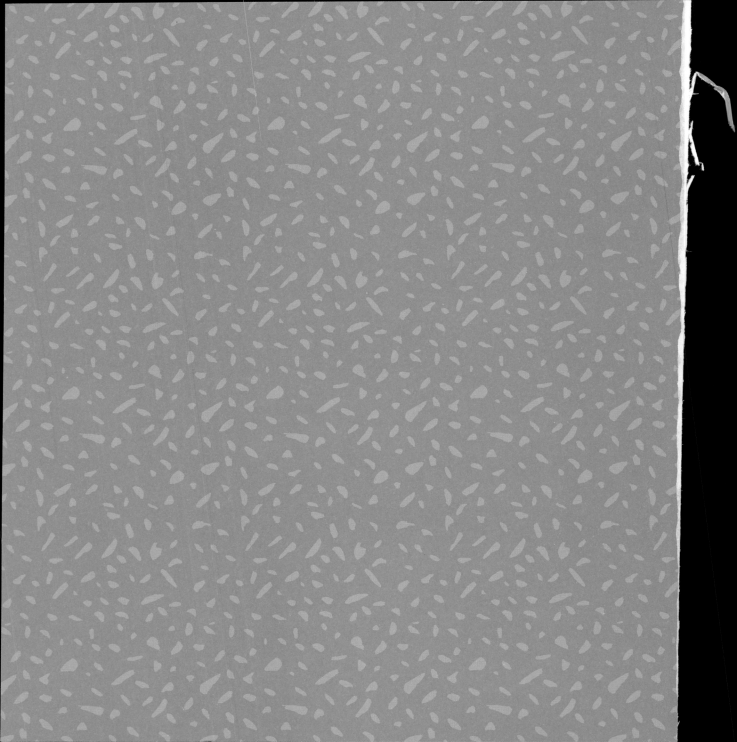

Easy Gingerbread Houses

Easy Gingerbread Houses

LISA TURNER ANDERSON

PHOTOGRAPHS BY ZAC WILLIAMS

GIBBS SMITH
TO ENRICH AND INSPIRE HUMANKIND

For Matt and Malcolm

First Edition
22 21 20 19 18   5 4 3 2 1

Text © 2018 Lisa Turner Anderson
Photographs © 2018 Zac Williams

Published by
Gibbs Smith
P.O. Box 667
Layton, Utah 84041

1.800.835.4993 orders
www.gibbs-smith.com

Designed by Kate Frances Design
Printed and bound in Hong Kong

Gibbs Smith books are printed on either recycled, 100% post-consumer
waste, FSC-certified papers or on paper produced from sustainable PEFC-
certified forest/controlled wood source. Learn more at www.pefc.org.

Library of Congress Cataloging-in-Publication Data
Names: Anderson, Lisa Turner, author.
Title: Easy gingerbread houses / Lisa Turner Anderson.
Description: Layton, Utah : Gibbs Smith, [2018]
Identifiers: LCCN 2018000366 | ISBN 9781423650348
(jacketless hardcover)
Subjects: LCSH: Gingerbread houses. | LCGFT: Cookbooks.
Classification: LCC TX771 .A5756 2018 | DDC 641.86/54—
dc23 LC record available at https://lccn.loc.gov/2018000366

Contents

Getting Started

Making no-bake gingerbread houses is easy, fun, and best of all, fast! This book will show you how to make houses, castles, cottages, and more using graham crackers, cookies, ice cream cones, waffle bowls, and candy. There's no need to mix dough, roll it out, bake it, and wait for it to harden. The house structures in this book take only minutes to make, meaning you can get to the decorating more quickly—and that's the best part.

Where to Build the House

A large piece of cardboard—at least 1 foot by 1 foot—is the best base to build your house on. It's sturdy enough to pick up so that you can move your house easily. Be sure to cover your cardboard with waxed paper or aluminum foil so the frosting doesn't seep through.

Even if the house is small and doesn't take up much room on the cardboard, you'll still want a large base so that you have plenty of room for decorating. The instructions for most of the houses in this book suggest that you spread icing around the house, such as green for grass or white for snow. Covering the whole cardboard base with icing helps your house look nice and neat.

Graham Crackers

While not all the houses in this book are made with graham crackers, most of them are. Building structures out of graham crackers requires a few tricks.

Most houses in the book require that you cut the graham crackers into shapes or smaller pieces. Instead of trying to break them with your hands, use a serrated knife, such as a steak or bread knife, to gently saw the cracker along the lines until the unwanted piece breaks off. If you try to break them with your hands, the pieces will usually break off unevenly.

The diagrams for each house will show you the sizes and shapes of the graham crackers you need. The blue parts of the diagram are the pieces of the crackers that need to be cut off and thrown away.

For many of the houses, you will need to glue 2 or more graham crackers together with icing to make a larger front, side, back, or roof piece. To help the pieces stay together, you will need to glue 1 quarter graham cracker across the seam, as shown in Diagram 1. This will help you make larger and more interesting houses without worrying about them falling apart. When you put the house together, make sure the reinforcing crackers are on the inside of the house.

Royal Icing

Making gingerbread houses requires special icing called royal icing. It is made with egg whites, water, and powdered sugar, and is very strong, like glue. It dries to a hard candy-like finish that will last for months. You can use either raw egg whites or meringue powder (which has dried egg whites) to make the icing. While both versions make equally strong icing, I prefer using meringue powder because it's easier to use and safer to eat than raw egg whites. You can find meringue powder at craft or cake decorating stores.

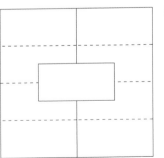

DIAGRAM 1

Egg White Royal Icing

Makes 4 cups

3 egg whites
½ teaspoon cream of tartar
4 cups powdered sugar

In a large, clean bowl, beat the egg whites and cream of tartar together until the meringue has formed stiff peaks. Beat in the sugar, 1 cup at a time, until mixed together and smooth.

Meringue Powder Royal Icing

Makes 4 cups

¼ cup meringue powder
½ cup water
4 cups powdered sugar

In a large, clean bowl, beat the meringue powder and water together until the meringue has formed stiff peaks. Beat in the sugar, 1 cup at a time, until mixed together and smooth.

TINTING

Tinting the icing with food coloring is a fun and easy way to add more color to your houses. Gel food coloring works the best because it is super concentrated and makes deep, bright colors. You can find gel food coloring in most grocery stores, but the gels at craft and cake decorating stores come in many more colors and are even more concentrated.

When tinting your icing, use a craft stick or toothpick to add just a tiny bit of gel to the icing. A little bit goes a very long way. You can always keep adding more, but you can't add less.

PIPING

The easiest way to use the icing to decorate your house is to spoon some of the frosting into a quart-size ziplock bag. Squeeze the air out of the top, then seal the bag. Double-check and make sure it is completely sealed or else the icing will come out the top when you squeeze the bag. Cut off a bottom corner of the bag and squeeze the bag to push the icing through the

hole. The smaller the hole, the thinner the line will be when you're piping the icing. You'll usually want a thinner line when decorating, but you can use a thicker line when gluing the house together.

If you want to get a little more creative with the frosting, use pastry bags with your favorite tip such as an open star tip, a leaf tip, or a ruffle tip, to add a decorative border where the edges have been glued together, or icicles hanging from the roof. Fill and keep a few bags ready with different tips and colors of icing. Any icing that is left in the bowl needs to be covered with plastic wrap so that the plastic wrap is touching the surface of the icing. Icing that is exposed to air will turn hard quickly and you won't be able to use it. This goes for the ziplock or pastry bags filled with icing as well. You don't want the tips to dry out.

You can store royal icing in the fridge for a few days.

Candy and More

The projects in this book have suggestions of what kind of candy, cookies, cereal, or even pretzels to use so that your house looks the same as the one in the photo. But if you have an idea for a different color or shape of candy or edible decoration for the house you're making, go for it! The best part of making gingerbread houses is using your imagination and playing with different candies to come up with a cool design that's all your own. You can use any candy you want, with one exception: taffy. After taffy is unwrapped, it will eventually "melt" and run down the sides of your house. Trust me—it doesn't look good!

Making a Sturdy House

Nothing is more frustrating than your gingerbread house falling down mid-decorating. These tips will help you make a sturdier structure.

- Make sure the icing is the right consistency. Icing that is too dry won't adhere well to graham crackers. If it's too dry, put it back in a bowl and beat in water, one tablespoon at a time, until the icing sticks well to the crackers.

- Make sure you glue the graham cracker walls to the cardboard base as well as to each other.

- Put a line of icing on each cracker when joining two together.

- Save the roof decorating for last. If the roof is weighed down too early with candy, it may slide off before the icing is hard enough to hold.

- If all of the above isn't working, let the house dry overnight before decorating.

Now that you know some tips, tricks, and important information, go have some fun, be creative, and build some really cool no-bake gingerbread houses.

The Houses

Easy Candy Cottage

ICING
1 batch white royal icing
  (see page 11)

GRAHAM CRACKERS (SEE DIAGRAMS)
2 vertical points
4 whole crackers

DECORATIONS
Sour Skittles
jelly fruit slices
candy canes
peppermints
gumdrops

Using royal icing, glue the house together with the vertical point crackers for the front and back and 2 whole crackers for the sides.

Pipe royal icing along the slanted lines of the point crackers. Glue the 2 remaining whole crackers on the slanted edges to form the roof. Pipe a line of icing along the top of the roof and gently push the roof pieces together.

Once the frosting has hardened and the house is sturdy, decorate as desired.

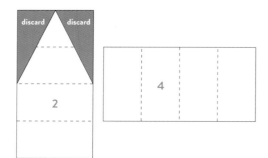

Lollipop Lane

GRAHAM CRACKERS (SEE DIAGRAMS)
7 half crackers, per house
2 quarter crackers, per house

ICING
1 batch white royal icing (see page 11)

DECORATIONS
orange jelly fruit slices
Starbursts
candy sticks
lollipops
jelly beans
jelly fruit slices

Cut 1 of the half crackers diagonally to make 2 triangles. Using royal icing, glue 1 triangle to the top of 1 half cracker to form the front of the house. Glue 1 quarter cracker across the seam to reinforce the 2 pieces. Repeat to make the back piece.

Assemble the house using the triangle-topped pieces you just made for the front and back of the house and 1 half cracker for each side. Pipe icing along the slanted rooflines and place 2 half crackers on top for the roof.

Repeat to make 2 more houses.

Once the frosting has hardened and the houses are sturdy, decorate as desired. To make orange bricks, cut orange jelly fruit slices into rectangles. To make the sidewalk squares, flatten purple Starburst candies and lay them in a row. Use a sharp pair of scissors to cut the candy sticks to the length of the house.

7 X 3

2 X 3

Sweetheart Cottage

GRAHAM CRACKERS (SEE DIAGRAMS)
8 whole crackers
2 bottom pieces
6 quarter crackers

ICING
½ batch white royal icing (see page 11)
½ batch brown royal icing (see Tinting, page 12)

DECORATIONS
large red hearts
small red and pink hearts

To make the front of the house, cut 1 whole cracker in half diagonally to make 2 long skinny triangles. Using white icing, glue the triangles together along the long straight edges. Glue 1 quarter cracker across the seam. Glue this piece to the long edge of 1 bottom piece. Then glue 2 quarter crackers across the seam.

Repeat to create the back of the house.

Put the house together using the front and back pieces and 2 whole crackers for the sides. Glue 2 whole crackers on each side for the roof.

Cover the front, back, and sides with brown icing. Decorate the front with the large candy hearts and piped icing. Cover the roof with white icing and decorate with small candy hearts. Pipe a decorative border on the edges, if desired.

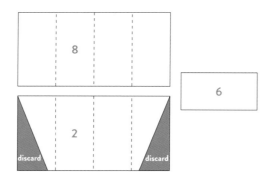

Fairy Tree House

ICING
1 batch royal icing
  (see page 11)

TREE HOUSE
16 (3-inch) molasses cookies
2 large flat-bottom waffle
  bowls, such as Joy or
  Kroger
about 40 spearmint leaves
Necco wafers
jelly beans

DECORATIONS
sour straws
gumdrops
chocolate pebbles
blue decorating sugar

Using icing, glue 8 cookies together in a stack. Glue a waffle bowl upside down on top of the stack. Repeat with the 8 remaining cookies and second waffle bowl to make a second stack.

Cut each spearmint leaf in half so that you have 2 thin leaves. Stick leaves in a row along the bottom edge of one of the waffle bowls. (The leaves should be sticky enough that you won't have to use icing.) Add a second row of leaves above the first row, staggering them. Keep making rows until the waffle bowl is completely covered. Repeat with the second waffle bowl. Glue the second stack on top of the first. If the tree is leaning, adjust it to straighten.

Glue wafers to the tree for windows, then pipe on window frames. Pipe a door at the bottom center of the tree and add a jelly bean doorknob.

Make a cobblestone path using speckled jelly beans. Use sour straws cut into small pieces for grass. Use pieces of gumdrops to make mushrooms. Use chocolate pebbles and blue sugar to make the brook.

Easter Bunny House

ICING
⅓ batch white royal icing
(see page 11)
⅓ batch yellow royal icing
(see Tinting, page 12)
⅓ batch green royal icing

GRAHAM CRACKERS (SEE DIAGRAMS)
6 three-quarter crackers
6 quarter crackers
2 vertical points

DECORATIONS
Necco wafers
jelly beans
flower confetti
gumdrops
Dum-Dums
spearmint leaves
chocolate sandwich cookies
candy corn

To make the front of the house, use white icing to glue 2 three-quarter crackers together along the longer edges. Glue a quarter cracker across the seam to reinforce the 2 pieces. Repeat to make the back of the house.

To make one side of the house, glue 1 quarter cracker to the bottom of a vertical point piece. Glue 1 quarter cracker across the seam to reinforce the 2 pieces. Glue the front, back, and sides together to make the house. Glue the remaining three-quarter crackers on top to make the roof.

Cover the house with yellow icing. Glue wafers to the roof for shingles. Make windows using different colors of jelly beans and pipe white icing for the window frames. Pipe a door using white icing and use a jelly bean for the doorknob. Pipe icing in front of the door to create a path, and sprinkle flower confetti over top, lightly pressing into the icing. Spread green frosting around the house to make the yard. Glue gumdrops, Dum-Dums, and spearmint leaves around the house to make flowers.

To make the carrot garden, crush cookies and sprinkle them in a square section of the yard. Cut the yellow and white parts off the candy corn, leaving the orange as the carrot. Make a little dent in the top of each carrot and insert a green piece of flower confetti. Place the carrots in rows in the dirt.

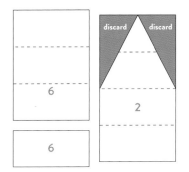

Mermaid Palace

ICING
⅓ batch white royal icing
(see page 11)
⅓ batch purple royal icing
(see Tinting, page 12)
⅔ batch seafoam-green
royal icing

PALACE
29 vanilla sandwich cookies
3 sugar cones
Smarties

DECORATIONS
sour gummy worms
gumdrops
green sour straws
candy seashells

To make the short tower, use white icing to glue 7 cookies together in a stack. Glue 1 sugar cone upside down on top. Repeat to make the middle tower, using 10 cookies. Repeat to make the tall tower, using 12 cookies.

Cover the tower tops with purple icing and the tower bottoms with green icing. Make the windows using Smarties for the windowpanes and pipe purple icing for the window frames.

Make sea anemones using gummy worms cut in half. Make a sea sponge using upside-down gumdrops. Make seaweed using sour straws.

Dutch Windmill

ICING
⅓ batch white royal icing
  (see page 11)
⅓ batch dark brown royal
  icing (see Tinting, page 12)
⅓ batch green royal icing

GRAHAM CRACKERS (SEE DIAGRAM)
5 windmill sides

WINDMILL
1 small waffle bowl, such as
  Keebler
4 chocolate sugar wafer
  cookies

DECORATIONS
gumdrops
green sour straws
spearmint leaves

Using white icing, make the bottom of the windmill by gluing the 5 windmill sides together to form a tower. The wide edges should be at the bottom and the narrow edges should meet at the top. Glue the waffle bowl upside down over the top.

Gently separate the top layer from each wafer cookie. Throw away or eat the bottom layers that have the frosting on them. Cover the windmill in brown icing, then stick the wafer tops to the windmill top to make the sails. Using white icing, pipe an X to connect the wafers.

Pipe on the windows using white icing. Make tulips by cutting gumdrops in half and sticking each half upside down onto a piece of sour straw. Use pieces of gumdrops instead of icing to glue the tulips together. Use spearmint leaves or sliced green gumdrops to make the tulip plant leaves. Spread green icing around the windmill to make the meadow. Stick the tulips into the green icing.

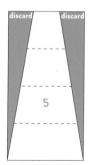

Cozy Cabin

ICING
1 batch white royal icing (see page 11), 1/2 cup reserved

GRAHAM CRACKERS (SEE DIAGRAMS, PAGE 32)
6 whole crackers
12 quarter crackers
8 three-quarter crackers
2 horizontal points

DECORATIONS
44 Pepperidge Farm Mint Chocolate Pirouette cookies
Pretzel sticks
Graham sticks
Sugar cones
spearmint leaves

Using royal icing, make one side of the roof by gluing 3 whole crackers together in a row along the long edges. Glue a quarter cracker across each seam to reinforce the pieces. Repeat to make the second side of the roof. Set aside both roof pieces to dry.

To make the front of the house, glue 2 three-quarter crackers together along the longer sides. Glue the long side of a horizontal point piece along the top of the 2 crackers. Glue a quarter cracker across each seam to reinforce the pieces. Repeat to make the back of the house.

Make one side of the house by gluing 2 three-quarter crackers together along the long edges. Glue a quarter cracker across the seams. Repeat to make the second side.

Glue the 4 sides together to make the house, making sure that the quarter seam crackers are on the inside of the house.

Glue a cookie along the bottom of the house front for the logs. One end of the cookie should be even with the left edge of the house and the other end should stick out past the right edge. Glue another cookie on top of the first cookie, staggering it so that the end sticks out past the left edge. Keep adding cookies this way on all sides of the house. You will need to cut some of the cookies to fit the top front and top back of the house.

CONTINUED . . .

Cozy Cabin

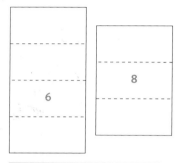

Pipe icing along the slanted rooflines and gently place each roof piece on top of the house, making sure the quarter seam crackers are on the inside. Cover the roof with icing and pipe icicles to the front eaves.

Make the windows and door out of pretzel sticks. Tint reserved icing dark yellow (see Tinting, page 12) and fill in the windowpanes. Glue graham sticks upside down to make the steps.

To make a pine tree, glue a sugar cone upside down next to the cabin. Cut spearmint leaves into 2 layers and stick the layers in rows around the cone. Repeat to make a second pine tree. Pipe some white frosting on the trees for snow, if desired.

Big Red Barn

ICING
¼ batch white royal icing (see page 11)
¼ batch red royal icing (see Tinting, page 12)
¼ batch brown royal icing
¼ batch green royal icing

GRAHAM CRACKERS (SEE DIAGRAMS, PAGE 34)
12 whole crackers
6 quarter crackers
2 barn tops

DECORATIONS
pretzel sticks
black licorice drops
yellow chocolate-covered sunflower seeds
brown M&Ms
green sour straws
green gumdrops

To make the front of the barn, use white icing to glue 2 whole crackers together on the long edges. Glue 1 quarter cracker across the seam to help the 2 pieces stay together. Glue 1 of the barn top graham crackers to the top. Then glue 1 quarter cracker across the seam. Repeat to make the back of the barn.

To make one side of the barn, glue 2 whole crackers together along the long edges. Glue 1 quarter cracker across the seam. Repeat to make the second side.

Put together the barn using the front and back pieces and the sides. Glue 2 whole crackers against the top slanted edges of the barn top pieces. Glue the 2 remaining whole crackers to the open slanted edges to complete the roof.

Cover the barn front and sides with red icing, reserving a little for later use. Pipe doors on the barn front using white icing. Cover the roof with brown icing. Spread the green icing around the barn for grass.

Make a sheep by sticking 4 pretzel sticks into 4 licorice drops. Break off the bottoms of the sticks until you have the desired height of the sheep. Glue the 4 drops together. To make the head, stick a pretzel stick into another licorice drop and stick this into the sheep. Cut pieces of drops for the ears and stick them to the head. Pipe dots of white

CONTINUED . . .

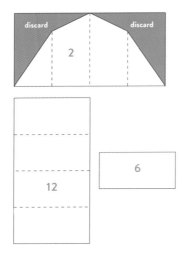

icing onto the sheep's body for fleece. Repeat to make a second sheep.

Make a sunflower by gluing sunflower seeds to the back of a brown M&M using the brown icing. Cut a sour straw in half lengthwise and glue it to the back of the sunflower. Repeat to make as many sunflowers as desired. Let dry overnight then glue the sunflowers to the barn using reserved red icing. Make leaves from green gumdrops and stick to the sunflower stems.

If you are feeling ambitious, make a fence with pretzel sticks and brown icing as shown in the photo. Make sure the icing is completely dried before standing up. Use green icing to glue the fence to the base.

Caribbean Bungalow

ICING
$2/3$ batch white royal icing
(see page 11)
$1/3$ batch yellow royal icing
(see Tinting, page 12)

GRAHAM CRACKERS (SEE DIAGRAMS)
4 whole crackers
4 half crackers

DECORATIONS
9 pretzel nuggets
Pretzel sticks
1 small waffle bowl, such as
Keebler
Shredded Wheat cereal
Andes Mints
Fruit Stripe Gum
blue decorating sugar
pretzel rods
spearmint leaves
vanilla wafer cookies

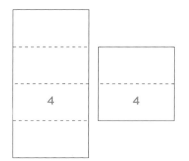

To make the platform, use white icing to glue 2 whole crackers together along the long edges. Glue 2 more whole crackers on top in the opposite direction. You should have a square platform with 2 cracker layers.

Glue pretzel bites to the platform in 3 evenly spaced rows of 3; these will be the feet for the base of the platform. Make sure they are all the same length so the platform will sit evenly. Gently turn the platform over and glue it, using the white icing, to a cardboard base.

Cover the top and sides of the platform with white icing and an even layer of pretzel sticks.

Using the white icing, make the bungalow on top of the platform by gluing 4 half crackers together. Glue the waffle bowl upside down on top of the bungalow.

Cover the bungalow in yellow icing and glue pieces of Shredded Wheat to the roof.

Make windows and a door using Andes Mints and white icing. Use pieces of the gum for the shutters. Spread the sugar underneath and around the platform. Make palm trees using pretzel rods and spearmint leaves. Stick the ends of the trees into more spearmint leaves and stick them to the cardboard base. Crush vanilla wafers to make sand, and spread around the palm trees to make the beach.

The Old Woman Who Lived in a Shoe

ICING
2/3 batch purple royal icing
(see page 11, and see
Tinting, page 12)
1/3 batch green royal icing

SHOE
13 (2 3/4-inch) soft bakery
cookies

GRAHAM CRACKERS (SEE DIAGRAM)
3 half crackers

DECORATIONS
green licorice snaps
yellow Chiclets
rainbow Airheads Xtremes
green sour straws
gumdrops

Using the purple icing, glue 8 cookies together in a stack. This will make the main part of the shoe. Cut the remaining cookies in half. Glue 6 cookie halves together in a stack. Turn the stack flat side down and place it against the stack of whole cookies. Glue 3 cookie halves together in a stack. Place this little stack at the end of the sideways stack to make the toe of the boot.

To make the roof, cut 1 half cracker in half diagonally to make 2 triangle pieces. Glue 1 triangle piece upright on top of the cookie stack, at the back. Glue the second triangle on top at the front of the stack. Glue 1 half cracker on each side to make the roof.

Frost the entire shoe, except the roof, with purple icing. Glue licorice snaps to the roof using green icing. Use green icing to pipe shoelaces.

Make the windows using yellow Chiclets for the windowpanes and Airheads Xtremes for the shutters. Make grass from sour straws cut into small pieces. Use bits of gumdrops to stick the grass to the shoe. Make mushrooms from pieces of red and white gumdrops.

3

Swiss Chalet

ICING
¾ batch brown royal icing
(see Tinting, page 12)
¼ batch white royal icing
(see page 11)

GRAHAM CRACKERS (SEE DIAGRAMS)
8 whole crackers
6 quarter crackers
2 horizontal points
4 three-quarter crackers

DECORATIONS
white Smarties
green gum
flower confetti
red heart confetti
Tootsie Rolls
spearmint leaves

To make the front of the house, use brown icing to glue 2 whole crackers together along the long edges. Glue 1 quarter cracker across the seam. Glue 1 horizontal point cracker along the top of the top cracker. Then glue 1 quarter cracker across the seam. Repeat to make the back of the house.

To make one side of the house, glue 2 three-quarter crackers together along the long edges. Glue 1 quarter cracker across the seam. Repeat to make the second side of the house.

Put the house together using the front, back, and side pieces. Glue 2 whole crackers on each side for the roof. Cover the entire house and roof with brown icing.

Glue Smarties in a row underneath the roof eaves. Pipe brown icing along the top of the Smarties. Pipe on the windows using white icing. Make shutters using gum and white flower confetti. Make window boxes using Tootsie Rolls cut in half. Glue green flower confetti and heart confetti to the window boxes. Pipe on designs using white icing. Slice spearmint leaves in half lengthwise and stack to make bushes.

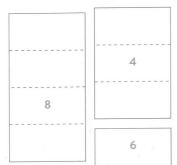

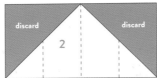

Firehouse

GRAHAM CRACKERS (SEE DIAGRAMS)
18 whole crackers
16 quarter crackers

ICING
3/4 batch white royal icing (see page 11) 1/2 cup reserved
1/4 batch dark brown royal icing (see Tinting, page 12)

DECORATIONS
Twizzlers Cherry Nibs
Andes Mints
mini Oreo cookies
cinnamon candies

To make the front of the firehouse, cut 1 whole cracker in half diagonally to make 2 long triangles. Using the white icing, glue the triangles together along the short edges. Glue 1 quarter cracker across the seam. Glue the short edges of 3 whole crackers along the bottom of this piece. Glue 1 quarter cracker across each seam. Repeat to make the back.

To make one side of the firehouse, glue 2 whole crackers together along the long edges. Glue 1 quarter cracker across the seam. Repeat to make the second side.

Glue the front, back, and sides together to make the firehouse.

To make the roof, glue 2 whole crackers together along the long edges. Glue 1 quarter cracker across the seam. Repeat to make the second roof piece. Carefully glue the roof pieces to the top of the firehouse.

Cover the roof with brown icing. Add the bricks to the sides and back of the firehouse by covering a portion of the wall with white icing, then arranging rows of Nibs to look like bricks. Continue doing small portions at a time, until the back and sides are covered.

To make the front, place bricks on the sides and top of the wall, leaving the middle uncovered. Cover the middle with

CONTINUED . . .

18

16

white icing, then make garage door windows using 4 Andes Mints. Make a brick border around the garage door.

To make the fire engine, cut 2 whole crackers in half lengthwise to make 4 long skinny pieces. Cut 1 piece widthwise into 3 equal pieces. Make the truck using 1 long skinny piece for the bottom and gluing 1 long skinny piece on each side. Glue 2 of the little pieces for the ends. (Discard the third little piece.) Glue a stack of 3 Andes Mints across the top at the front end of the truck, about $1/2$ inch from the front edge. Lean 1 Andes Mint against the front side of the stack. Tint reserved icing red and cover the entire truck. Pipe details using white icing. Make wheels using Oreos and cinnamon candies.

Blue Dollhouse

GRAHAM CRACKERS (SEE DIAGRAMS PAGE 46)

ICING
⅓ batch white royal icing (see page 11)
⅓ batch light blue royal icing (see Tinting, page 12)
⅓ batch green royal icing

GRAHAM CRACKERS (SEE DIAGRAMS PAGE 46)
7 whole crackers
4 quarter crackers
4 half crackers
2 vertical points

DECORATIONS
Andes Mints
candy sticks
white Smarties
orange licorice snaps
spearmint leaves
large green gumdrops
flower confetti

To make the front of the house, use white icing to glue 2 whole crackers together along the long edges. Glue 1 quarter cracker across the seam to reinforce the pieces. Repeat to make the back of the house.

To make one side of the house, glue 1 half cracker to the bottom of 1 vertical point piece. Glue 1 quarter cracker across the seam. Repeat to make the second side.

Glue the front, back, and sides together to make the house. Glue 1 whole cracker on each side for the roof.

To make the gable, cut 2 half crackers in half diagonally to make 4 triangle pieces. Throw away the fourth triangle. Pipe icing along the bottom side of 1 triangle and hold it gently at the bottom front of the roof. Still holding the triangle, pipe icing along the top two sides of the triangle. Glue a triangle perpendicular to each side of the first triangle. The opposite edges of the second and third triangles should meet at the top. Pipe icing along this top seam and along the bottom edges of the second and third triangles, where they meet the roof.

Frost the whole house, except the roof, in blue icing. Make windows using pieces of Andes Mints and white icing. Pipe the door using white icing.

CONTINUED . . .

Blue Dollhouse

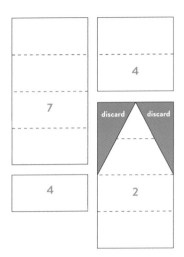

To make the porch, cut 1 whole cracker in half lengthwise to make 2 long skinny pieces. Glue 1 piece along the bottom of the house. Cover the porch in white icing. Break the candy sticks into pieces about 2 1/2 inches long. Glue 2 sticks on either end of the porch for pillars. Glue the second long skinny cracker piece to the house so that it rests on top of the candy sticks. Lift up the porch roof gently and glue 2 more candy sticks to the porch.

Decorate the roof and porch roof using white icing and Smarties. Make a brick path using pieces of orange licorice snaps and white icing. Make flower bushes using pieces of spearmint leaves, gumdrops, and confetti. Spread green icing around the house to make the yard.

Mushroom Gnome Home

(see page 11)

ICING
1/2 batch off-white royal
  icing (see page 11)
1/4 batch red royal icing (see
  Tinting, page 12)
1/4 batch brown royal icing

MUSHROOM
8 (3-inch) cookies
1 small waffle bowl, such as
  Keebler
Necco Wafers
Tootsie Rolls

DECORATIONS
pretzel sticks
red heart confetti
chocolate pebbles
flower confetti
green sour straws
speckled jelly beans

Using off-white icing, glue the cookies together in a stack. Glue the waffle bowl upside down on top of the stack.

Cover the top of the mushroom with red icing. Place white wafers on top to make spots.

Cover the mushroom stem with off-white icing. Using brown icing, pipe a door on the front. Place a wafer on each side of the door for windows. Pipe thin lines of brown icing around the wafers to create window frames.

Shape a Tootsie Roll into a chimney and glue it at the back of the roof using red icing.

Make the mailbox using a pretzel stick stuck into a Tootsie Roll and a heart confetti for the flag. Use chocolate pebbles for rocks, flower confetti for flowers, and sour straws cut into small pieces for grass. Use jelly beans for the cobblestone path.

Igloo

ICING
1 batch white royal icing
  (see page 11)

IGLOO
Sugar cubes

DECORATIONS
white gumdrops
Twizzlers black licorice Nibs
black jelly beans
orange gumdrops
blue decorating sugar

To make the first layer of the igloo, use icing to glue 22 sugar cubes in a circle. Building upwards, make more layers using fewer sugar cubes each time until you just have 1 cube at the top. As you make the layers, glue down the cubes with icing and spread the cubes out evenly along the layer beneath.

Make the entrance to the igloo using 3 layers of 2 cubes on each side. Cover the top and fill in the gaps between all the cubes with icing.

Make the penguins by cutting the tops and sides off white gumdrops to reveal the sticky inside. Make wings from pieces of licorice and heads from black jelly beans cut in half. Make feet and beaks using pieces of orange gumdrops.

Spread icing around the igloo and arrange the penguins in the icing. Sprinkle blue decorating sugar on one side of the igloo to make the ocean.

Seven Dwarfs' Cottage

2 half crackers
12 quarter crackers
12 whole crackers
2 vertical points
2 three-quarter crackers

ICING
3/4 batch off-white royal
  icing (see page 11)
1/4 batch dark brown royal
  icing (see Tinting, page 12)

DECORATIONS
Tootsie Rolls
Corn Chex cereal
Andes Mints
pretzel sticks
Twizzlers black licorice Nibs
flower or heart confetti
rock candy

To make the right half of the house, follow the assembly directions for the Easy Candy Cottage (see page 16).

To make the front door piece, cut 1 half cracker in half diagonally to make 2 triangle pieces. Using off-white icing, glue 1 triangle to 1 half cracker. Glue 1 quarter cracker across the seam. Set aside.

Glue 1 quarter cracker perpendicular to the front of the house, a fourth of the way in from the right side. Then glue another quarter cracker perpendicular to the front of the house, a fourth of the way in from the left side. Glue the second triangle across the 2 quarter pieces where the quarter pieces meet the roof. Glue the triangle-topped piece that you had set aside to the open ends of the 2 quarter crackers. Glue the last 2 quarter crackers on top of the structure to make a roof.

Cover the house and door piece with off-white icing. Add the cereal squares to the roof and over the door piece. Pipe a door on the front door piece using brown icing.

Shape 2 Tootsie Rolls into tree trunks. Glue 1 quarter cracker above the door and use the tree trunks to hold up the porch roof. Cover the quarter cracker with frosting.

CONTINUED . . .

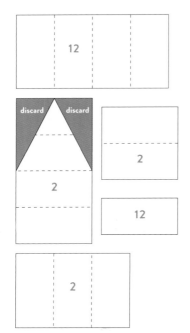

To make the front of the left half of the house, cut 1 whole cracker in half diagonally to make 2 long skinny triangles. Glue the triangles together along the long straight edges. Glue 1 quarter cracker across the seam. Glue this piece to the long edge of a whole cracker. Then glue 2 quarter crackers across the seam.

Repeat to make the back of the house.

Build the left half of the house using the front and back pieces and 1 horizontal three-quarter cracker for each side. Glue 2 whole crackers on each side for the roof.

Cover the left half of the house with off-white icing. Glue the cereal squares on both sides of the roof for shingles. Position the houses together as shown in the photo. Use brown icing to pipe on the woodwork for both sections of the house. Use Andes Mints for the windows and Tootsie Rolls for the shutters. Glue white confetti onto the shutters. Make pickaxes by cutting crescent shapes from licorice and sticking them to pretzel sticks. Decorate yard with rock candy for jewels.

Haunted Mansion

GRAHAM CRACKERS (SEE DIAGRAMS, PAGE 56)
11 half crackers
11 whole crackers
11 quarter crackers
4 Haunted Mansion Tops

ICING
1/3 batch white royal icing (see page 11) 1/2 cup reserved
1/3 batch dark purple royal icing (see Tinting, page 12)
1/3 batch orange royal icing

DECORATIONS
purple Chiclets
orange Chiclets
purple fruit slices
yellow Chiclets
black licorice twists and laces
orange M&Ms
pumpkin candies
gummy spiders

To make the right tower of the house, cut 1 half cracker in half diagonally to make 2 triangles. Using white icing, glue 1 triangle to the short edge of 1 whole cracker. Glue 1 quarter cracker across the seam. Repeat to make a second triangle-topped piece. Make the tower by gluing the triangle-topped side pieces to 1 whole cracker for the front and another whole cracker for the back. Glue 2 half crackers to the slanted eaves to make the roof.

Repeat to make the left tower.

To make the center tower, glue 1 half cracker to 1 whole cracker along the short edges. Glue 1 quarter cracker across the seam. Repeat 3 times to make 4 long pieces. Glue the 4 long pieces together to make the tower.

Glue the 4 Haunted Mansion Top graham crackers together along the slanted lines to make a pyramid shape with a flat top. Then glue the last half cracker on top of the flat pyramid. Glue the flat pyramid on top of the center tower.

Glue the shorter towers to each side of the tall tower, about halfway back so that the tall tower sticks out in front of the side towers.

Cut about 1/2 inch off the ends of 3 quarter graham crackers. Make a porch by stacking 2 of these crackers at

CONTINUED . . .

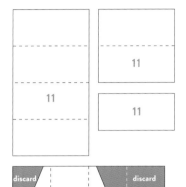

the base of the front tower. Set aside the remaining cracker to make the porch roof later.

Frost the entire house, except the roof, in purple icing. While the icing is still wet, make windowpanes out of purple Chiclets and purple fruit slices and make shutters out of orange Chiclets. Use orange Chiclets for the front door.

Cut 2 pieces of black licorice to about $2\frac{1}{2}$ inches each. Cover the cut quarter cracker you set aside earlier with purple icing. Attach the porch roof above the door and prop it up using the black licorice pieces.

Cover the entire roof with orange icing, and press in orange M&Ms for the shingles. Make the roof railing by cutting licorice laces into small pieces and some long strips and sticking them into the icing.

Glue yellow Chiclets to the center front of the roof. Tint the reserved frosting black and pipe around the window frames. Glue pumpkins and gummy spiders around the house.

Santa's Castle

ICING
½ batch off-white royal
   icing (see page 11)
¼ batch red icing (see
   Tinting, page 12)
¼ batch green icing

GRAHAM CRACKERS (SEE DIAGRAMS, PAGE 60)
12 whole crackers
11 quarter crackers
4 half crackers

TOWERS
16 vanilla sandwich cookies
2 sugar cones

DECORATIONS
yellow Chiclets
yellow fruit slices
green sour straws
Fruit Stripe Gum
cinnamon candies
apple gummy ring
spearmint leaves
waffle cone
Sour Skittles
peppermints
peppermint candy stick
Big Red gum

To make the front of the castle, use off-white icing to glue 3 whole crackers together along the long edges. Glue 1 quarter cracker across each seam. Repeat with 3 more whole crackers and 2 quarter crackers to make the back of the castle.

To make the sides of the castle, cut 1 half cracker in half diagonally to make 2 triangle pieces. To make one side, glue 1 triangle to 1 whole cracker along the short edge. Glue 1 quarter cracker across the seam. Repeat to make the second side.

Glue the front, back, and sides together to make the castle.

To make the roof, glue 1 half cracker to 1 whole cracker along the short edge. Glue 1 quarter cracker across the seam. Repeat to make the other side of the roof. Pipe icing along the slanted rooflines. Carefully place the long roof pieces on top of the slanted rooflines.

To make the front part of the house, cut 1 half cracker in half diagonally to make 2 triangle pieces. Glue 1 triangle to 1 whole cracker along the short edge. Glue 1 quarter cracker across the seam. Cut 1 whole cracker in half lengthwise to make 2 long skinny pieces. Glue each long piece perpendicular to the front of the house, one-third of the way in from the left side and one-third of the way in

CONTINUED . . .

Santa's Castle

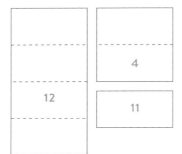

from the right side. Glue the triangle-topped whole cracker to the long skinny crackers. Glue the second triangle piece at the top back of the long skinny pieces. Pipe icing along the slanted lines. Glue 1 quarter cracker on each side to make the little roof.

To make a tower, use off-white icing to glue 8 cookies together in a stack. Glue a sugar cone to the top. Repeat to make a second tower. Place a tower on each side of the castle.

Cover the castle with off-white icing and the roof and tower tops with red icing. Make windows using yellow Chiclets, yellow fruit slices, red icing, and sour straws. Make the front door using 2 pieces of red gum, cutting the top corners into a rounded shape. Add a cinnamon candy for a doorknob and an apple gummy ring for a wreath. Make garlands across the rooflines using green icing.

Make bushes using spearmint leaves. Make a tree using an upside-down waffle cone and thin layers of spearmint leaves. Glue Skittles to the tree for ornaments. Make a path in front of the house using peppermints. Make a North Pole sign using a peppermint candy stick and a piece of Big Red gum wrapped around the top. Pipe "North Pole" on the gum using white icing.

Dracula's Castle

ICING
¾ batch dark gray royal
  icing (see page 11 and
  see Tinting, page 12)
¼ batch black royal icing
A few tablespoons yellow
  royal icing

GRAHAM CRACKERS (SEE DIAGRAMS, PAGE 63)
13 whole crackers
4 vertical points
6 half crackers
6 quarter crackers

HILL
5 flat-bottom waffle bowls,
  such as Joy or Kroger

ROUND TOWERS
1 package vanilla wafer
  cookies
12 sandwich cookies
2 sugar cones
1 waffle cone

DECORATIONS
black licorice twists and
  Nibs
Tootsie Rolls
yellow Chiclets

Make the hill by using gray royal icing to glue 4 waffle bowls upside down in a square onto your cardboard base. Glue 1 whole cracker across the front and back bowls on the right side of the square and another whole cracker across the front and back bowls on the left side. Then glue 1 whole cracker across the 2 front bowls, on top of the other two crackers, and 1 whole cracker across the two back bowls. Glue a third cracker between the two front and back crackers. You should now have 3 whole crackers lying on top of 2 whole crackers.

To make the front of the short rectangle tower, glue 1 half cracker to the bottom of 1 vertical point cracker. Glue 1 quarter cracker across the seam. Repeat to make the back of the tower. Build the tower at the front of the hill, using the front and back pieces you have just made and 2 whole crackers for the side pieces. Make the roof using 2 half crackers.

To make the front of the tall back tower, glue the short side of 1 whole cracker to the bottom of 1 point cracker. Glue 1 quarter cracker across the seam. Repeat to make the back of the tower. Make each side by gluing 2 whole crackers together along the short edges. Glue 1 quarter cracker across the seam. Build the tower at the back left of the hill, using the front and back pieces and the side pieces you have just made. Make the roof using 2 half crackers.

CONTINUED . . .

Dracula's Castle

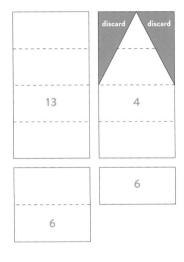

Make the left round tower by gluing 7 vanilla wafers together in a stack; glue a sugar cone upside down on top of the stack. Repeat to make the right round tower, using 9 vanilla wafers. Repeat to make the back round tower, using the sandwich cookies and a waffle cone.

Create the path by making 5 stacks of vanilla wafers, using 6 wafers for one stack, 5 for the next, then 4, then 3, then 2. Arrange the stacks from tallest to shortest to make a path.

Cover the towers, hill, and path with gray icing. Cover the tower roofs with black icing.

Make the moon from a waffle bowl by gently breaking off the sides of the bowl so that the bottom circle remains. Cover the circle with yellow icing and stick it to the back of the tall left tower.

Cut bat shapes from black licorice twists and place on the moon. Make the front door using Tootsie Rolls and licorice Nibs, and pipe a circle on the front with black icing.

Make windows using Chiclets. Make trees by cutting the top half of licorice twists into strips and bending them outward. Glue the trees to the towers and the sides of the path.

Silly Polka-Dot House

ICING
½ batch green royal icing (see page 11 and see Tinting, page 12)
¼ batch purple royal icing
¼ batch blue royal icing

GRAHAM CRACKERS (SEE DIAGRAMS)
4 Silly Polka Dot A
5 half crackers
3 three-quarter crackers
2 Silly Polka Dot B

DECORATIONS
M&Ms
Spree candies

Using green icing, make the first floor of the house with 2 A crackers for the front and back of the house and 2 half crackers for the sides. Make sure the straight side of the front and back pieces is on the right and the slanted side is on the left. Glue 1 three-quarter cracker across the top.

Repeat to make the second floor, this time placing the straight side on the left and the slanted side on the right. Glue 1 three-quarter cracker across the top.

Make the top floor using the B pieces as the front and back, making sure the longer side of the triangle is on the left. Make the roof using 1 half cracker for the short right side and 1 three-quarter cracker for the long left side.

Cover the entire house in green icing. Pipe on windows and a door using purple icing, then outline in blue. Outline the sides of the house in blue. Decorate using M&Ms and Spree candies.

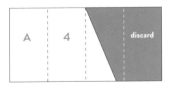

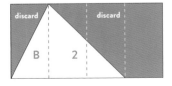

Pink Castle in the Clouds

ICING
1/3 batch white royal icing (see page 11)
1/3 batch pink royal icing (see Tinting, page 12)
1/3 batch purple royal icing

TOWERS
33 vanilla wafers
5 standard ice cream cones
5 waffle cones

GRAHAM CRACKERS (SEE DIAGRAMS)
6 three-quarters crackers
2 quarter crackers

DECORATIONS
purple jelly candy
pink candy sticks
pink gum
pink cotton candy

To make one front tower, use white icing to glue 5 vanilla wafers together in a stack. Glue the bottom of 1 ice cream cone to the top of the cookie stack. Repeat to make the second front tower.

Breaking off small pieces at a time, gently remove about 1 inch from the top rim of a waffle cone. (This will help it fit better into the ice cream cup.) Using a serrated knife, gently saw about 1 inch off the bottom of the cone to make a hole for the candy stick. Turn the waffle cone upside down and glue it into the top of the tower. Repeat for the second tower.

Repeat to make the two back towers, using 7 vanilla wafers for each tower. Make the center tower using 9 vanilla wafers. Be careful with the towers—they can easily fall down until they're stabilized.

To make the front of the castle, glue 2 three-quarter crackers together along the long sides. Glue 1 quarter cracker across the seam. Glue the two shortest towers to either side of the cracker wall.

Make each side of the castle by gluing 1 three-quarter cracker vertically between a short front tower and a medium back tower.

CONTINUED . . .

Pink Castle in the Clouds

Make the back of the castle by gluing the remaining 2 three-quarter crackers together along the long sides. Glue 1 quarter cracker across the seam. Glue this wall between the two back towers.

Place the tallest tower inside the castle and glue it against the back wall.

Cut brick shapes from purple jelly candy. Frost the entire castle except the waffle cones in pink icing. While the icing is still wet, stick the jelly bricks to the towers and walls. Pipe a castle gate using purple icing.

Cover the waffle cones with purple icing, then put a candy stick inside each waffle cone hole. Cut flag shapes out of gum and glue them to the top of each candy stick. Spread cotton candy around the base of the castle for clouds.

Tiki Hut

ICING

½ batch brown royal icing
(see Tinting, page 12)
½ batch white royal icing
(page 11) divided and
tinted hot pink, turquoise,
yellow, purple, and green

**GRAHAM CRACKERS (SEE
DIAGRAMS)**

2 horizontal points
5 whole crackers
4 quarter crackers
2 half crackers

DECORATIONS

Shredded Wheat cereal
Andes Mints
pretzel rods
spearmint leaves
pretzel sticks
orange gumdrops
vanilla wafer cookies

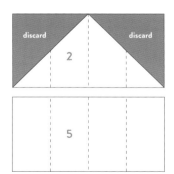

To make the front and back of the hut, use brown icing to glue 1 horizontal point cracker to a whole cracker along the long edges. Glue 1 quarter cracker across the seam to help the 2 pieces stay together. Repeat with the second triangle piece and another whole cracker.

To make the roof pieces, cut 1 whole cracker in half diagonally to make 2 long triangles. Glue 1 triangle to a whole cracker along the long edges. Glue 1 quarter cracker across the seam. Repeat to make a second roof piece.

Put together the hut using the front and back pieces and 2 half crackers for the sides. Glue the roof pieces on top, so that the shortest edge of the roof is at the bottom and the long pointed edges meet at the top.

Cover the hut, including the roof, with brown icing. Cover the roof with crushed pieces of Shredded Wheat.

Glue 2 Andes Mints horizontally to the front of the hut to make the door.

Using the different colors of icing, pipe a door frame and designs on the front of the hut. Pipe a tiki mask on either side of the door frame.

CONTINUED . . .

Tiki Hut

Make palm trees by gluing pretzel rods topped with pieces of spearmint leaves and position them next to the hut. Make bamboo torches using pretzel sticks with pieces of orange gumdrops stuck to the tops for the flames. Stick the torches into spearmint leaves and place them in front of the hut.

Crush the vanilla wafer cookies in a food processor to make sand. Spread the sand around the hut, making sure to cover the bottoms of the torches.

About the Author

Lisa Anderson is an editor, writer, baker, and stand-up comedienne whose keen sense of humor keeps her thinking outside the box. She has authored two books, and lives in Salt Lake City, UT.

Metric Conversion Chart

VOLUME MEASUREMENTS		WEIGHT MEASUREMENTS		TEMPERATURE CONVERSION	
U.S.	METRIC	U.S.	METRIC	FAHRENHEIT	CELSIUS
1 teaspoon	5 ml	1/2 ounce	15 g	250	120
1 tablespoon	15 ml	1 ounce	30 g	300	150
1/4 cup	60 ml	3 ounces	90 g	325	160
1/3 cup	75 ml	4 ounces	115 g	350	180
1/2 cup	125 ml	8 ounces	225 g	375	190
2/3 cup	150 ml	12 ounces	350 g	400	200
3/4 cup	175 ml	1 pound	450 g	425	220
1 cup	250 ml	2 1/4 pounds	1 kg	450	230

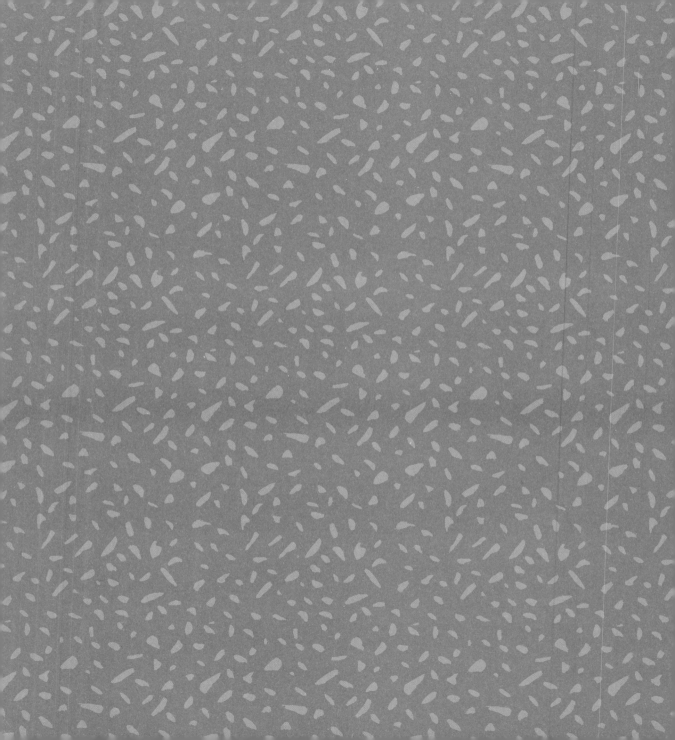